MznLnx

Missing Links Exam Preps

Exam Prep for

Selling Today: Creating Customer Value

Manning, Reece, & Reece, 10th Edition

The MznLnx Exam Prep is your link from the texbook and lecture to your exams.
The MznLnx Exam Preps are unauthorized and comprehensive reviews of your textbooks.

MznLnx

Rico
Publications

Exam Prep for Selling Today: Creating Customer Value
10th Edition
Manning, Reece, & Reece

Publisher: Raymond Houge
Assistant Editor: Michael Rouger
Text and Cover Designer: Lisa Buckner
Marketing Manager: Sara Swagger
Project Manager, Editorial Production: Jerry Emerson
Art Director: Vernon Lowerui

Product Manager: Dave Mason
Editorial Assitant: Rachel Guzmanji
Pedagogy: Debra Long
Cover Image: Jim Reed/Getty Images
Text and Cover Printer: City Printing, Inc.
Compositor: Media Mix, Inc.

For more information about our products, contact us at:
Dave.Mason@RicoPublications.com

For permission to use material from this text or product, submit a request online to:
Dave.Mason@RicoPublications.com

Printed in the United States
ISBN:

Contents

TO THE STUDENT

COMPREHENSIVE

The *MznLnx* Exam Prep series is designed to help you pass your exams. Editors at MznLnx review your textbooks and then prepare these practice exams to help you master the textbook material. Unlike study guides, workbooks, and practice tests provided by the texbook publisher and textbook authors, *MznLnx* gives you ***all*** of the material in each chapter in exam form, not just samples, so you can be sure to nail your exam.

MECHANICAL

The MznLnx Exam Prep series creates exams that will help you learn the subject matter as well as test you on your understanding. Each question is designed to help you master the concept. Just working through the exams, you gain an understanding of the subject--its a simple mechanical process that produces success.

INTEGRATED STUDY GUIDE AND REVIEW

MznLnx is not just a set of exams designed to test you, its also a comprehensive review of the subject content. Each exam question is also a review of the concept, making sure that you will get the answer correct without having to go to other sources of material. You learn as you go! Its the easiest way to pass an exam.

HUMOR

Studying can be tedious and dry. MznLnx's instructional design includes moderate humor within the exam questions on occassion, to break the tedium and revitalize the brain

1. _________ refers to the additional value of a commodity over the cost of commodities used to produce it from the previous stage of production. An example is the price of gasoline at the pump over the price of the oil in it. In national accounts used in macroeconomics, it refers to the contribution of the factors of production, i.e., land, labor, and capital goods, to raising the value of a product and corresponds to the incomes received by the owners of these factors. The factors of production provide 'services' which raise the unit price of a product (X) relative to the cost per unit of intermediate goods used up in the production of X. _________ is shared between the factors of production (capital, labor, also human capital), giving rise to issues of distribution.

a. Consumer spending
b. Power III
c. Deregulation
d. Value added

2. _________ is defined by the American _________ Association as the activity, set of institutions, and processes for creating, communicating, delivering, and exchanging offerings that have value for customers, clients, partners, and society at large. The term developed from the original meaning which referred literally to going to market, as in shopping, or going to a market to sell goods or services.

_________ practice tends to be seen as a creative industry, which includes advertising, distribution and selling.

a. Marketing myopia
b. Customer acquisition management
c. Product naming
d. Marketing

3. The _________ is generally accepted as the use and specification of the four p's describing the strategic position of a product in the marketplace. One version of the origins of the _________ starts in 1948 when James Culliton said that a marketing decision should be a result of something similar to a recipe. This version continued in 1953 when Neil Bordon, in his American Marketing Association presidential address, took the recipe idea one step further and coined the term 'Marketing-Mix'.

a. 6-3-5 Brainwriting
b. Marketing mix
c. 180SearchAssistant
d. Power III

4. _________ involves disseminating information about a product, product line, brand, or company. It is one of the four key aspects of the marketing mix. (The other three elements are product marketing, pricing, and distribution). P>_________ is generally sub-divided into two parts:

- Above the line _________: Promotion in the media (e.g. TV, radio, newspapers, Internet and Mobile Phones) in which the advertiser pays an advertising agency to place the ad
- Below the line _________: All other _________. Much of this is intended to be subtle enough for the consumer to be unaware that _________ is taking place. E.g. sponsorship, product placement, endorsements, sales _________, merchandising, direct mail, personal selling, public relations, trade shows

a. Promotion
b. Davie Brown Index
c. Cashmere Agency
d. Bottling lines

5. The term _________ was first coined by New York Times best selling author, Linda Richardson. _________ emphasizes customer needs and meeting those needs with solutions combining products and/or services. A consultative salesperson typically provides detailed instruction or advice on which solution best meets these needs.
a. Sales management
b. Consultative selling
c. Request for proposal
d. Lead generation

6. _________ is the identity of a group or culture, or of an individual as far as one is influenced by one's belonging to a group or culture. _________ is similar to and has overlaps with, but is not synonymous with, identity politics.

There are modern questions of culture that are transferred into questions of identity.

a. Cultural identity
b. 6-3-5 Brainwriting
c. Power III
d. 180SearchAssistant

7. _________ is an organization's process of defining its strategy and making decisions on allocating its resources to pursue this strategy, including its capital and people. Various business analysis techniques can be used in _________, including SWOT analysis (Strengths, Weaknesses, Opportunities, and Threats) and PEST analysis (Political, Economic, Social, and Technological analysis) or STEER analysis involving Socio-cultural, Technological, Economic, Ecological, and Regulatory factors and EPISTEL (Environment, Political, Informatic, Social, Technological, Economic and Legal)

_________ is the formal consideration of an organization's future course. All _________ deals with at least one of three key questions:

1. 'What do we do?'
2. 'For whom do we do it?'
3. 'How do we excel?'

In business _________, the third question is better phrased 'How can we beat or avoid competition?'. (Bradford and Duncan, page 1.)

a. 180SearchAssistant
b. 6-3-5 Brainwriting
c. Power III
d. Strategic planning

8. A _________ is a plan of action designed to achieve a particular goal.

_________ is different from tactics. In military terms, tactics is concerned with the conduct of an engagement while _________ is concerned with how different engagements are linked.

a. 180SearchAssistant
b. Power III
c. 6-3-5 Brainwriting
d. Strategy

9. _________ in organizations and public policy is both the organizational process of creating and maintaining a plan; and the psychological process of thinking about the activities required to create a desired goal on some scale. As such, it is a fundamental property of intelligent behavior. This thought process is essential to the creation and refinement of a plan, or integration of it with other plans, that is, it combines forecasting of developments with the preparation of scenarios of how to react to them.

a. Power III
b. 180SearchAssistant
c. Planning
d. 6-3-5 Brainwriting

10. _________ in economics and business is the result of an exchange and from that trade we assign a numerical monetary value to a good, service or asset. If I trade 4 apples for an orange, the _________ of an orange is 4 - apples. Inversely, the _________ of an apple is 1/4 oranges.

a. Contribution margin-based pricing
b. Discounts and allowances
c. Pricing
d. Price

11. _________, commonly known as e-commerce or eCommerce, consists of the buying and selling of products or services over electronic systems such as the Internet and other computer networks. The amount of trade conducted electronically has grown extraordinarily with wide-spread Internet usage. A wide variety of commerce is conducted in this way, spurring and drawing on innovations in electronic funds transfer, supply chain management, Internet marketing, online transaction processing, electronic data interchange (EDI), inventory management systems, and automated data collection systems.
a. ADTECH
b. AMAX
c. Electronic commerce
d. ACNielsen

12. _________ consists of the processes a company uses to track and organize its contacts with its current and prospective customers. _________ software is used to support these processes; information about customers and customer interactions can be entered, stored and accessed by employees in different company departments. Typical _________ goals are to improve services provided to customers, and to use customer contact information for targeted marketing.
a. Commercialization
b. Demand generation
c. Product bundling
d. Customer relationship management

13. Customer _________ consists of the processes a company uses to track and organize its contacts with its current and prospective customers. CRelationship management software is used to support these processes; information about customers and customer interactions can be entered, stored and accessed by employees in different company departments. Typical CRelationship management goals are to improve services provided to customers, and to use customer contact information for targeted marketing.
a. Marketing
b. Green marketing
c. Relationship management
d. Product bundling

14. _________ is a branch of philosophy which seeks to address questions about morality, such as how a moral outcome can be achieved in a specific situation (applied _________), how moral values should be determined (normative _________), what moral values people actually abide by (descriptive _________), what the fundamental semantic, ontological, and epistemic nature of _________ or morality is (meta-_________), and how moral capacity or moral agency develops and what its nature is (moral psychology.)

Socrates was one of the first Greek philosophers to encourage both scholars and the common citizen to turn their attention from the outside world to the condition of man. In this view, Knowledge having a bearing on human life was placed highest, all other knowledge being secondary.

a. ADTECH
b. ACNielsen
c. Ethics
d. AMAX

1. _________ is the provision of service to customers before, during and after a purchase.

According to Turban et al., '_________ is a series of activities designed to enhance the level of customer satisfaction - that is, the feeling that a product or service has met the customer expectation.'

Its importance varies by product, industry and customer.

a. COPC Inc.
b. Customer experience
c. Facing
d. Customer service

2. _________ is an advertisement in which a particular product specifically mentions a competitor by name for the express purpose of showing why the competitor is inferior to the product naming it.

This should not be confused with parody advertisements, where a fictional product is being advertised for the purpose of poking fun at the particular advertisement, nor should it be confused with the use of a coined brand name for the purpose of comparing the product without actually naming an actual competitor. ('Wikipedia tastes better and is less filling than the Encyclopedia Galactica.')

In the 1980s, during what has been referred to as the cola wars, soft-drink manufacturer Pepsi ran a series of advertisements where people, caught on hidden camera, in a blind taste test, chose Pepsi over rival Coca-Cola.

a. Comparative advertising
b. Cost per conversion
c. Heavy-up
d. GL-70

3. An _________ is a person who has possession of an enterprise and assumes significant accountability for the inherent risks and the outcome. It is an ambitious leader who combines land, labour, and capital to create and market new goods or services. The term is a loanword from French and was first defined by the Irish economist Richard Cantillon.
a. Entrepreneur
b. ADTECH
c. ACNielsen
d. AMAX

4. Importance of _________ is critical for any commercial organization. Expanding business is not possible without increasing sales volumes, and effective _________ goal is to organize sales team work in such a manner that ensures a growing flow of regular customers and increasing amount of sales.

The four phase-model of Management Process

1. Conception
2. Planning
3. Execution
4. Control

This model is cyclical, so it is a constant/continuous process.

===_________ is attainment of sales force goals in a effective ' efficient manner through planning, staffing, training, leading ' controlling organizational resources.

a. Sales management
b. Sales process
c. Hit rate
d. Request for proposal

5. _________ is a mathematical science pertaining to the collection, analysis, interpretation or explanation, and presentation of data. It also provides tools for prediction and forecasting based on data. It is applicable to a wide variety of academic disciplines, from the natural and social sciences to the humanities, government and business.

a. Median
b. Null hypothesis
c. Statistics
d. Type I error

6. _________ is a form of communication that typically attempts to persuade potential customers to purchase or to consume more of a particular brand of product or service. 'While now central to the contemporary global economy and the reproduction of global production networks, it is only quite recently that _________ has been more than a marginal influence on patterns of sales and production. The formation of modern _________ was intimately bound up with the emergence of new forms of monopoly capitalism around the end of the 19th and beginning of the 20th century as one element in corporate strategies to create, organize and where possible control markets, especially for mass produced consumer goods.

a. Advertising
b. AMAX
c. ACNielsen
d. ADTECH

7. _________ is a contract between two parties, one being the employer and the other being the employee. An employee may be defined as: 'A person in the service of another under any contract of hire, express or implied, oral or written, where the employer has the power or right to control and direct the employee in the material details of how the work is to be performed.' Black's Law Dictionary page 471 (5th ed. 1979.)

a. ADTECH
b. ACNielsen
c. Employment
d. AMAX

8. _________ is the identity of a group or culture, or of an individual as far as one is influenced by one's belonging to a group or culture. _________ is similar to and has overlaps with, but is not synonymous with, identity politics.

There are modern questions of culture that are transferred into questions of identity.

a. Power III
b. 180SearchAssistant
c. 6-3-5 Brainwriting
d. Cultural identity

9. Wholesaling, historically called jobbing, is the sale of goods or merchandise to retailers, to industrial, commercial, institutional or to other wholesalers and related subordinated services.

According to the United Nations Statistics Division, '_________' is the resale (sale without transformation) of new and used goods to retailers, to industrial, commercial, institutional or professional users or involves acting as an agent or broker in buying merchandise for such persons or companies. Wholesalers frequently physically assemble, sort and grade goods in large lots, break bulk, repack and redistribute in smaller lots.

a. Supply chain network
b. Supply network
c. Wholesale
d. Purchasing

10. _________ is a method of direct marketing in which a salesperson solicits to prospective customers to buy products or services, either over the phone or through a subsequent face to face or Web conferencing appointment scheduled during the call.

_________ can also include recorded sales pitches programmed to be played over the phone via automatic dialing. _________ has come under fire in recent years, being viewed as an annoyance by many.

a. Phishing
b. Directory Harvest Attack
c. Joe job
d. Telemarketing

11. _________ refers to the confirmation of certain characteristics of an object, person, or organization. This confirmation is often, but not always, provided by some form of external review, education, or assessment. One of the most common types of _________ in modern society is professional _________, where a person is certified as being able to competently complete a job or task, usually by the passing of an examination.

a. Power III
b. 6-3-5 Brainwriting
c. Certification
d. 180SearchAssistant

1. A _________ is a plan of action designed to achieve a particular goal.

_________ is different from tactics. In military terms, tactics is concerned with the conduct of an engagement while _________ is concerned with how different engagements are linked.

a. Power III
b. Strategy
c. 6-3-5 Brainwriting
d. 180SearchAssistant

2. A personal and cultural _________ is a relative ethic _________, an assumption upon which implementation can be extrapolated. A _________ system is a set of consistent _________s and measures that is soo not true. A principle _________ is a foundation upon which other _________s and measures of integrity are based.
a. Package-on-Package
b. Supreme Court of the United States
c. Value
d. Perceptual maps

3. _________ consists of the processes a company uses to track and organize its contacts with its current and prospective customers. _________ software is used to support these processes; information about customers and customer interactions can be entered, stored and accessed by employees in different company departments. Typical _________ goals are to improve services provided to customers, and to use customer contact information for targeted marketing.
a. Product bundling
b. Customer relationship management
c. Commercialization
d. Demand generation

4. _________ is a branch of philosophy which seeks to address questions about morality, such as how a moral outcome can be achieved in a specific situation (applied _________), how moral values should be determined (normative _________), what moral values people actually abide by (descriptive _________), what the fundamental semantic, ontological, and epistemic nature of _________ or morality is (meta-_________), and how moral capacity or moral agency develops and what its nature is (moral psychology.)

Socrates was one of the first Greek philosophers to encourage both scholars and the common citizen to turn their attention from the outside world to the condition of man. In this view, Knowledge having a bearing on human life was placed highest, all other knowledge being secondary.

a. ADTECH
b. Ethics
c. AMAX
d. ACNielsen

5. Customer _________ consists of the processes a company uses to track and organize its contacts with its current and prospective customers. CRelationship management software is used to support these processes; information about customers and customer interactions can be entered, stored and accessed by employees in different company departments. Typical CRelationship management goals are to improve services provided to customers, and to use customer contact information for targeted marketing.

a. Marketing
b. Green marketing
c. Product bundling
d. Relationship management

6. The term _________ was first coined by New York Times best selling author, Linda Richardson. _________ emphasizes customer needs and meeting those needs with solutions combining products and/or services. A consultative salesperson typically provides detailed instruction or advice on which solution best meets these needs.

a. Lead generation
b. Consultative selling
c. Request for proposal
d. Sales management

7. _________ is the identity of a group or culture, or of an individual as far as one is influenced by one's belonging to a group or culture. _________ is similar to and has overlaps with, but is not synonymous with, identity politics.

There are modern questions of culture that are transferred into questions of identity.

a. 6-3-5 Brainwriting
b. Power III
c. 180SearchAssistant
d. Cultural identity

1. _________ is a standard point of view or personal prejudice. especially when the tendency interferes with the ability to be impartial, unprejudiced, or objective. The term _________ed is used to describe an action, judgment, or other outcome influenced by a prejudged perspective.

a. 6-3-5 Brainwriting
b. 180SearchAssistant
c. Power III
d. Bias

2. _________ refer to a collection of facts usually collected as the result of experience, observation or experiment or a set of premises. This may consist of numbers, words particularly as measurements or observations of a set of variables. _________ are often viewed as a lowest level of abstraction from which information and knowledge are derived.

a. Mean
b. Sample size
c. Data
d. Pearson product-moment correlation coefficient

3. _________ is the identity of a group or culture, or of an individual as far as one is influenced by one's belonging to a group or culture. _________ is similar to and has overlaps with, but is not synonymous with, identity politics.

There are modern questions of culture that are transferred into questions of identity.

a. Cultural identity
b. 6-3-5 Brainwriting
c. Power III
d. 180SearchAssistant

1. _________ is a branch of philosophy which seeks to address questions about morality, such as how a moral outcome can be achieved in a specific situation (applied _________), how moral values should be determined (normative _________), what moral values people actually abide by (descriptive _________), what the fundamental semantic, ontological, and epistemic nature of _________ or morality is (meta-_________), and how moral capacity or moral agency develops and what its nature is (moral psychology.)

Socrates was one of the first Greek philosophers to encourage both scholars and the common citizen to turn their attention from the outside world to the condition of man. In this view, Knowledge having a bearing on human life was placed highest, all other knowledge being secondary.

a. ACNielsen
b. ADTECH
c. Ethics
d. AMAX

2. _________ is the identity of a group or culture, or of an individual as far as one is influenced by one's belonging to a group or culture. _________ is similar to and has overlaps with, but is not synonymous with, identity politics.

There are modern questions of culture that are transferred into questions of identity.

a. 6-3-5 Brainwriting
b. 180SearchAssistant
c. Power III
d. Cultural identity

3. The _________ of 1977 (15 U.S.C. Â§Â§ 78dd-1, et seq.) is a United States federal law known primarily for two of its main provisions, one that addresses accounting transparency requirements under the Securities Exchange Act of 1934 and another concerning bribery of foreign officials.

a. Trademark dilution
b. Tenth Amendment
c. Copyright
d. Foreign Corrupt Practices Act

4. In the social sciences, a _________ is a society where valuable goods and services are regularly given without any explicit agreement for immediate or future rewards (i.e. there is no visible quid pro quo). Ideally, simultaneous or recurring giving serves to circulate and redistribute valuables within the community. The organization of a _________ stands in contrast to a barter economy or a market economy.

a. Gift economy
b. Protectionism
c. Black market
d. Mixed economy

5. In law, _________ also called calumny, libel for written words, slander for spoken words, is the communication of a statement that makes a claim, expressly stated or implied to be factual, that may give an individual, business, product, group, government or nation a negative image. It is usually, but not always, a requirement that this claim be false and that the publication is communicated to someone other than the person defamed

In common law jurisdictions, slander refers to a malicious, false and defamatory spoken statement or report, while libel refers to any other form of communication such as written words or images.

a. Muckraker
b. Free trade zone
c. Free good
d. Defamation

6. _________ is a form of communication that typically attempts to persuade potential customers to purchase or to consume more of a particular brand of product or service. 'While now central to the contemporary global economy and the reproduction of global production networks, it is only quite recently that _________ has been more than a marginal influence on patterns of sales and production. The formation of modern _________ was intimately bound up with the emergence of new forms of monopoly capitalism around the end of the 19th and beginning of the 20th century as one element in corporate strategies to create, organize and where possible control markets, especially for mass produced consumer goods.

a. AMAX
b. Advertising
c. ACNielsen
d. ADTECH

7. _________ is the provision of service to customers before, during and after a purchase.

According to Turban et al., '_________ is a series of activities designed to enhance the level of customer satisfaction - that is, the feeling that a product or service has met the customer expectation.'

Its importance varies by product, industry and customer.

a. Customer experience
b. COPC Inc.
c. Facing
d. Customer service

8. _________ is an advertisement in which a particular product specifically mentions a competitor by name for the express purpose of showing why the competitor is inferior to the product naming it.

This should not be confused with parody advertisements, where a fictional product is being advertised for the purpose of poking fun at the particular advertisement, nor should it be confused with the use of a coined brand name for the purpose of comparing the product without actually naming an actual competitor. ('Wikipedia tastes better and is less filling than the Encyclopedia Galactica.')

In the 1980s, during what has been referred to as the cola wars, soft-drink manufacturer Pepsi ran a series of advertisements where people, caught on hidden camera, in a blind taste test, chose Pepsi over rival Coca-Cola.

a. GL-70
b. Cost per conversion
c. Heavy-up
d. Comparative advertising

9. A personal and cultural _________ is a relative ethic _________, an assumption upon which implementation can be extrapolated. A _________ system is a set of consistent _________s and measures that is soo not true. A principle _________ is a foundation upon which other _________s and measures of integrity are based.
a. Perceptual maps
b. Package-on-Package
c. Supreme Court of the United States
d. Value

10. The _________ is an independent agency of the United States government, established in 1914 by the _________ Act. Its principal mission is the promotion of 'consumer protection' and the elimination and prevention of what regulators perceive to be harmfully 'anti-competitive' business practices, such as coercive monopoly.

The _________ Act was one of President Wilson's major acts against trusts.

a. Power III
b. Federal Trade Commission
c. 6-3-5 Brainwriting
d. 180SearchAssistant

1. A _________ is a plan of action designed to achieve a particular goal.

_________ is different from tactics. In military terms, tactics is concerned with the conduct of an engagement while _________ is concerned with how different engagements are linked.

a. 6-3-5 Brainwriting
b. 180SearchAssistant
c. Power III
d. Strategy

2. _________ is the physical search for minerals, fossils, precious metals or mineral specimens, and is also known as fossicking.

_________ is synonymous in some ways with mineral exploration which is an organised, large scale and at least semi-scientific effort undertaken by mineral resource companies to find commercially viable ore deposits. To actually be considered a prospector you must become registered as a professional prospector.

a. 180SearchAssistant
b. Power III
c. 6-3-5 Brainwriting
d. Prospecting

3. In engineering and manufacturing, _________ is involved in developing systems to ensure products or services are designed and produced to meet or exceed customer requirements or SLA's. Genetic algorithms are search techniques, used in computing to find exact or approximate solutions to optimization and search problems.

Alternative _________ procedures can be applied on a process to test statistically the null hypothesis, that the process is in control, against the alternative, that the process is out of control.

a. 180SearchAssistant
b. 6-3-5 Brainwriting
c. Power III
d. Quality control

4. _________ refer to a collection of facts usually collected as the result of experience, observation or experiment or a set of premises. This may consist of numbers, words particularly as measurements or observations of a set of variables. _________ are often viewed as a lowest level of abstraction from which information and knowledge are derived.

a. Sample size
b. Mean
c. Pearson product-moment correlation coefficient
d. Data

5. A _________ is an explicit set of requirements to be satisfied by a material, product, or service.

In engineering, manufacturing, and business, it is vital for suppliers, purchasers, and users of materials, products, or services to understand and agree upon all requirements. A _________ is a type of a standard which is often referenced by a contract or procurement document.

a. New product development
b. Specification
c. Product optimization
d. Product development

6. _________ is the provision of service to customers before, during and after a purchase.

According to Turban et al., '_________ is a series of activities designed to enhance the level of customer satisfaction - that is, the feeling that a product or service has met the customer expectation.'

Its importance varies by product, industry and customer.

a. COPC Inc.
b. Customer service
c. Facing
d. Customer experience

7. _________ is an advertisement in which a particular product specifically mentions a competitor by name for the express purpose of showing why the competitor is inferior to the product naming it.

This should not be confused with parody advertisements, where a fictional product is being advertised for the purpose of poking fun at the particular advertisement, nor should it be confused with the use of a coined brand name for the purpose of comparing the product without actually naming an actual competitor. ('Wikipedia tastes better and is less filling than the Encyclopedia Galactica.')

In the 1980s, during what has been referred to as the cola wars, soft-drink manufacturer Pepsi ran a series of advertisements where people, caught on hidden camera, in a blind taste test, chose Pepsi over rival Coca-Cola.

a. Heavy-up
b. Comparative advertising
c. Cost per conversion
d. GL-70

8. _________ is one of the four Ps of the marketing mix. The other three aspects are product, promotion, and place. It is also a key variable in microeconomic price allocation theory.
a. Relationship based pricing
b. Competitor indexing
c. Price
d. Pricing

9. _________ is a term that refers both to:

- a formal discipline used to help appraise, or assess, the case for a project or proposal, which itself is a process known as project appraisal; and
- an informal approach to making decisions of any kind.

Under both definitions the process involves, whether explicitly or implicitly, weighing the total expected costs against the total expected benefits of one or more actions in order to choose the best or most profitable option. The formal process is often referred to as either CBA (_________) or BCost-benefit analysis

A hallmark of CBA is that all benefits and all costs are expressed in money terms, and are adjusted for the time value of money, so that all flows of benefits and flows of project costs over time (which tend to occur at different points in time) are expressed on a common basis in terms of their 'present value.' Closely related, but slightly different, formal techniques include Cost-effectiveness analysis, Economic impact analysis, Fiscal impact analysis and Social Return on Investment(SROI) analysis. The latter builds upon the logic of _________, but differs in that it is explicitly designed to inform the practical decision-making of enterprise managers and investors focused on optimising their social and environmental impacts.

a. Cost-benefit analysis
b. 180SearchAssistant
c. 6-3-5 Brainwriting
d. Power III

10. A _________ is a collection of symbols, experiences and associations connected with a product, a service, a person or any other artifact or entity.

_________s have become increasingly important components of culture and the economy, now being described as 'cultural accessories and personal philosophies'.

Some people distinguish the psychological aspect of a _________ from the experiential aspect.

a. Brand equity
b. Store brand
c. Brandable software
d. Brand

11. _________ is a service provided by many retailers of various products, primarily electronics, that provides the end-user with a resource for information regarding the product, and help if the product should malfunction. _________ can be found in most manuals for products in the form of a phone number, website address, or physical location.

The Internet has allowed for a new form of _________ to develop.

a. Psychological pricing
b. Product life cycle
c. Price-weighted
d. Product support

12. _________ is a rivalry between individuals, groups, nations for territory, a niche, or allocation of resources. It arises whenever two or more parties strive for a goal which cannot be shared. _________ occurs naturally between living organisms which co-exist in the same environment.

a. Price competition
b. Price fixing
c. Non-price competition
d. Competition

13. _________ is the identity of a group or culture, or of an individual as far as one is influenced by one's belonging to a group or culture. _________ is similar to and has overlaps with, but is not synonymous with, identity politics.

There are modern questions of culture that are transferred into questions of identity.

a. Power III
b. Cultural identity
c. 6-3-5 Brainwriting
d. 180SearchAssistant

14. _________ is a branch of philosophy which seeks to address questions about morality, such as how a moral outcome can be achieved in a specific situation (applied _________), how moral values should be determined (normative _________), what moral values people actually abide by (descriptive _________), what the fundamental semantic, ontological, and epistemic nature of _________ or morality is (meta-_________), and how moral capacity or moral agency develops and what its nature is (moral psychology.)

Socrates was one of the first Greek philosophers to encourage both scholars and the common citizen to turn their attention from the outside world to the condition of man. In this view, Knowledge having a bearing on human life was placed highest, all other knowledge being secondary.

a. Ethics
b. ADTECH
c. ACNielsen
d. AMAX

1. In marketing, _________ has come to mean the process by which marketers try to create an image or identity in the minds of their target market for its product, brand, or organization. It is the 'relative competitive comparison' their product occupies in a given market as perceived by the target market.

Re-_________ involves changing the identity of a product, relative to the identity of competing products, in the collective minds of the target market.

a. Moratorium
b. Containerization
c. GE matrix
d. Positioning

2. A personal and cultural _________ is a relative ethic _________, an assumption upon which implementation can be extrapolated. A _________ system is a set of consistent _________s and measures that is soo not true. A principle _________ is a foundation upon which other _________s and measures of integrity are based.

a. Supreme Court of the United States
b. Perceptual maps
c. Value
d. Package-on-Package

3. _________ is a branch of philosophy which seeks to address questions about morality, such as how a moral outcome can be achieved in a specific situation (applied _________), how moral values should be determined (normative _________), what moral values people actually abide by (descriptive _________), what the fundamental semantic, ontological, and epistemic nature of _________ or morality is (meta-_________), and how moral capacity or moral agency develops and what its nature is (moral psychology.)

Socrates was one of the first Greek philosophers to encourage both scholars and the common citizen to turn their attention from the outside world to the condition of man. In this view, Knowledge having a bearing on human life was placed highest, all other knowledge being secondary.

a. ADTECH
b. AMAX
c. ACNielsen
d. Ethics

4. _________ is a rivalry between individuals, groups, nations for territory, a niche, or allocation of resources. It arises whenever two or more parties strive for a goal which cannot be shared. _________ occurs naturally between living organisms which co-exist in the same environment.

a. Competition
b. Price competition
c. Price fixing
d. Non-price competition

5. _________ is one of the four Ps of the marketing mix. The other three aspects are product, promotion, and place. It is also a key variable in microeconomic price allocation theory.
a. Relationship based pricing
b. Competitor indexing
c. Price
d. Pricing

6. _________ in economics and business is the result of an exchange and from that trade we assign a numerical monetary value to a good, service or asset. If I trade 4 apples for an orange, the _________ of an orange is 4 - apples. Inversely, the _________ of an apple is 1/4 oranges.
a. Discounts and allowances
b. Pricing
c. Contribution margin-based pricing
d. Price

7. _________ is the provision of service to customers before, during and after a purchase.

According to Turban et al., '_________ is a series of activities designed to enhance the level of customer satisfaction - that is, the feeling that a product or service has met the customer expectation.'

Its importance varies by product, industry and customer.

a. Customer experience
b. Customer service
c. COPC Inc.
d. Facing

8. In engineering and manufacturing, _________ is involved in developing systems to ensure products or services are designed and produced to meet or exceed customer requirements or SLA's. Genetic algorithms are search techniques, used in computing to find exact or approximate solutions to optimization and search problems.

Alternative _________ procedures can be applied on a process to test statistically the null hypothesis, that the process is in control, against the alternative, that the process is out of control.

a. 6-3-5 Brainwriting
b. 180SearchAssistant
c. Quality control
d. Power III

9. _________ is an advertisement in which a particular product specifically mentions a competitor by name for the express purpose of showing why the competitor is inferior to the product naming it.

This should not be confused with parody advertisements, where a fictional product is being advertised for the purpose of poking fun at the particular advertisement, nor should it be confused with the use of a coined brand name for the purpose of comparing the product without actually naming an actual competitor. ('Wikipedia tastes better and is less filling than the Encyclopedia Galactica.')

In the 1980s, during what has been referred to as the cola wars, soft-drink manufacturer Pepsi ran a series of advertisements where people, caught on hidden camera, in a blind taste test, chose Pepsi over rival Coca-Cola.

a. Cost per conversion
b. Heavy-up
c. GL-70
d. Comparative advertising

10. _________ is a form of communication that typically attempts to persuade potential customers to purchase or to consume more of a particular brand of product or service. 'While now central to the contemporary global economy and the reproduction of global production networks, it is only quite recently that _________ has been more than a marginal influence on patterns of sales and production. The formation of modern _________ was intimately bound up with the emergence of new forms of monopoly capitalism around the end of the 19th and beginning of the 20th century as one element in corporate strategies to create, organize and where possible control markets, especially for mass produced consumer goods.

a. AMAX
b. ACNielsen
c. ADTECH
d. Advertising

11. _________ is the identity of a group or culture, or of an individual as far as one is influenced by one's belonging to a group or culture. _________ is similar to and has overlaps with, but is not synonymous with, identity politics.

There are modern questions of culture that are transferred into questions of identity.

a. Power III
b. 6-3-5 Brainwriting
c. 180SearchAssistant
d. Cultural identity

12. _________ refers to the additional value of a commodity over the cost of commodities used to produce it from the previous stage of production. An example is the price of gasoline at the pump over the price of the oil in it. In national accounts used in macroeconomics, it refers to the contribution of the factors of production, i.e., land, labor, and capital goods, to raising the value of a product and corresponds to the incomes received by the owners of these factors. The factors of production provide 'services' which raise the unit price of a product (X) relative to the cost per unit of intermediate goods used up In the production of X. _________ is shared between the factors of production (capital, labor, also human capital), giving rise to issues of distribution.
a. Value added
b. Power III
c. Deregulation
d. Consumer spending

13. _________ are infrequent, technical, or unique functions performed by independent contractors or consultants whose occupation is the rendering of such services. Examples of _________ contracts include: accountants, actuaries, appraisers, archaeologists, architects, attorneys, brokerage firms, business consultants, business development managers, copywriters, engineers, law firms, physicians, public relations professionals, recruiters, researchers, real estate brokers, translators, software engineers and web designers. While not limited to licentiates (individuals holding professional licenses), the services are considered 'professional' and the contract may run to partnerships, firms, or corporations as well as to individuals.
a. Professional services
b. Spokesperson
c. 180SearchAssistant
d. Power III

1. _________ is the physical search for minerals, fossils, precious metals or mineral specimens, and is also known as fossicking.

_________ is synonymous in some ways with mineral exploration which is an organised, large scale and at least semi-scientific effort undertaken by mineral resource companies to find commercially viable ore deposits. To actually be considered a prospector you must become registered as a professional prospector.

a. Power III
b. Prospecting
c. 6-3-5 Brainwriting
d. 180SearchAssistant

2. In economics, business, retail, and accounting, a _________ is the value of money that has been used up to produce something, and hence is not available for use anymore. In economics, a _________ is an alternative that is given up as a result of a decision. In business, the _________ may be one of acquisition, in which case the amount of money expended to acquire it is counted as _________.

a. Transaction cost
b. Variable cost
c. Fixed costs
d. Cost

3. A _________ is a plan of action designed to achieve a particular goal.

_________ is different from tactics. In military terms, tactics is concerned with the conduct of an engagement while _________ is concerned with how different engagements are linked.

a. Strategy
b. Power III
c. 6-3-5 Brainwriting
d. 180SearchAssistant

4. _________ is a broad label that refers to any individuals or households that use goods and services generated within the economy. The concept of a _________ is used in different contexts, so that the usage and significance of the term may vary.

A _________ is a person who uses any product or service.

a. 6-3-5 Brainwriting
b. Consumer
c. Power III
d. 180SearchAssistant

5. _________ is a term that has been used in various psychology theories, often in slightly different ways (e.g., Goldstein, Maslow, Rogers.) The term was originally introduced by the organismic theorist Kurt Goldstein for the motive to realise all of one's potentialities. In his view, it is the master motive--indeed, the only real motive a person has, all others being merely manifestations of it.
a. Self-actualization
b. 180SearchAssistant
c. Power III
d. 6-3-5 Brainwriting

6. A _________ is a sociological concept referring to a group to which an individual or another group is compared.

_________s are used in order to evaluate and determine the nature of a given individual or other group's characteristics and sociological attributes. It is the group to which the individual relates or aspires relate himself or self psychologically.

a. Reference group
b. Minority
c. Power III
d. Mociology

7. In sociology, anthropology and cultural studies, a _________ is a group of people with a culture (whether distinct or hidden) which differentiates them from the larger culture to which they belong. If a particular _________ is characterized by a systematic opposition to the dominant culture, it may be described as a counterculture. As Ken Gelder notes, _________s are social, with their own shared conventions, values and rituals, but they can also seem 'immersed' or self-absorbed--another feature that distinguishes them from countercultures.
a. Power III
b. Subculture
c. 6-3-5 Brainwriting
d. 180SearchAssistant

8. _________ is the identity of a group or culture, or of an individual as far as one is influenced by one's belonging to a group or culture. _________ is similar to and has overlaps with, but is not synonymous with, identity politics.

There are modern questions of culture that are transferred into questions of identity.

a. 6-3-5 Brainwriting
b. 180SearchAssistant
c. Power III
d. Cultural identity

1. _________ is the physical search for minerals, fossils, precious metals or mineral specimens, and is also known as fossicking.

_________ is synonymous in some ways with mineral exploration which is an organised, large scale and at least semi-scientific effort undertaken by mineral resource companies to find commercially viable ore deposits. To actually be considered a prospector you must become registered as a professional prospector.

a. Power III
b. 180SearchAssistant
c. 6-3-5 Brainwriting
d. Prospecting

2. _________ in organizations and public policy is both the organizational process of creating and maintaining a plan; and the psychological process of thinking about the activities required to create a desired goal on some scale. As such, it is a fundamental property of intelligent behavior. This thought process is essential to the creation and refinement of a plan, or integration of it with other plans, that is, it combines forecasting of developments with the preparation of scenarios of how to react to them.
a. 180SearchAssistant
b. 6-3-5 Brainwriting
c. Power III
d. Planning

3. A trade fair (trade show or expo) is an exhibition organized so that companies in a specific industry can showcase and demonstrate their latest products, service, study activities of rivals and examine recent trends and opportunities. Some trade fairs are open to the public, while others can only be attended by company representatives (members of the trade) and members of the press, therefore _________ are classified as either 'Public' or 'Trade Only'. They are held on a continuing basis in virtually all markets and normally attract companies from around the globe.
a. 180SearchAssistant
b. Power III
c. 6-3-5 Brainwriting
d. Trade shows

4. _________ is a method of direct marketing in which a salesperson solicits to prospective customers to buy products or services, either over the phone or through a subsequent face to face or Web conferencing appointment scheduled during the call.

_________ can also include recorded sales pitches programmed to be played over the phone via automatic dialing. _________ has come under fire in recent years, being viewed as an annoyance by many.

a. Phishing
b. Telemarketing
c. Directory Harvest Attack
d. Joe job

5. _________ is a form of communication that typically attempts to persuade potential customers to purchase or to consume more of a particular brand of product or service. 'While now central to the contemporary global economy and the reproduction of global production networks, it is only quite recently that _________ has been more than a marginal influence on patterns of sales and production. The formation of modern _________ was intimately bound up with the emergence of new forms of monopoly capitalism around the end of the 19th and beginning of the 20th century as one element in corporate strategies to create, organize and where possible control markets, especially for mass produced consumer goods.

a. ADTECH
b. ACNielsen
c. AMAX
d. Advertising

6. _________ is the process of approaching prospective customers or clients, typically via telephone, who were not expecting such an interaction. The word 'cold' is used because the person receiving the call is not expecting a call or has not specifically asked to be contacted by a sales person.

Within the United Kingdom, the Privacy and Electronic Communications (EC Directive) Regulations 2003 make it unlawful to transmit an automated recorded message for direct marketing purposes via a telephone, without prior consent of the subscriber.

a. Power III
b. Database marketing
c. Cold calling
d. Direct Marketing Associations

7. An _________ is a special-purpose computer system designed to perform one or a few dedicated functions, often with real-time computing constraints. It is usually embedded as part of a complete device including hardware and mechanical parts. In contrast, a general-purpose computer, such as a personal computer, can do many different tasks depending on programming.

a. ADTECH
b. ACNielsen
c. AMAX
d. Embedded system

8. A _________ is a structured collection of records or data that is stored in a computer system. The structure is achieved by organizing the data according to a _________ model. The model in most common use today is the relational model.

a. Power III
b. 180SearchAssistant
c. 6-3-5 Brainwriting
d. Database

9. _________ is a branch of philosophy which seeks to address questions about morality, such as how a moral outcome can be achieved in a specific situation (applied _________), how moral values should be determined (normative _________), what moral values people actually abide by (descriptive _________), what the fundamental semantic, ontological, and epistemic nature of _________ or morality is (meta-_________), and how moral capacity or moral agency develops and what its nature is (moral psychology.)

Socrates was one of the first Greek philosophers to encourage both scholars and the common citizen to turn their attention from the outside world to the condition of man. In this view, Knowledge having a bearing on human life was placed highest, all other knowledge being secondary.

a. ACNielsen
b. AMAX
c. ADTECH
d. Ethics

10. _________ is the identity of a group or culture, or of an individual as far as one is influenced by one's belonging to a group or culture. _________ is similar to and has overlaps with, but is not synonymous with, identity politics.

There are modern questions of culture that are transferred into questions of identity.

a. 180SearchAssistant
b. Power III
c. 6-3-5 Brainwriting
d. Cultural identity

1. A _________ is a plan of action designed to achieve a particular goal.

_________ is different from tactics. In military terms, tactics is concerned with the conduct of an engagement while _________ is concerned with how different engagements are linked.

a. 180SearchAssistant
b. 6-3-5 Brainwriting
c. Power III
d. Strategy

2. A personal and cultural _________ is a relative ethic _________, an assumption upon which implementation can be extrapolated. A _________ system is a set of consistent _________s and measures that is soo not true. A principle _________ is a foundation upon which other _________s and measures of integrity are based.

a. Supreme Court of the United States
b. Package-on-Package
c. Perceptual maps
d. Value

3. _________ is a branch of philosophy which seeks to address questions about morality, such as how a moral outcome can be achieved in a specific situation (applied _________), how moral values should be determined (normative _________), what moral values people actually abide by (descriptive _________), what the fundamental semantic, ontological, and epistemic nature of _________ or morality is (meta-_________), and how moral capacity or moral agency develops and what its nature is (moral psychology.)

Socrates was one of the first Greek philosophers to encourage both scholars and the common citizen to turn their attention from the outside world to the condition of man. In this view, Knowledge having a bearing on human life was placed highest, all other knowledge being secondary.

a. ACNielsen
b. AMAX
c. Ethics
d. ADTECH

4. _________ in organizations and public policy is both the organizational process of creating and maintaining a plan; and the psychological process of thinking about the activities required to create a desired goal on some scale. As such, it is a fundamental property of intelligent behavior. This thought process is essential to the creation and refinement of a plan, or integration of it with other plans, that is, it combines forecasting of developments with the preparation of scenarios of how to react to them.

a. 180SearchAssistant
b. Planning
c. 6-3-5 Brainwriting
d. Power III

5. _________ is a form of social influence. It is the process of guiding people toward the adoption of an idea, attitude, or action by rational and symbolic (though not always logical) means. It is strategy of problem-solving relying on 'appeals' rather than coercion.

a. Power III
b. 6-3-5 Brainwriting
c. 180SearchAssistant
d. Persuasion

6. _________ is the identity of a group or culture, or of an individual as far as one is influenced by one's belonging to a group or culture. _________ is similar to and has overlaps with, but is not synonymous with, identity politics.

There are modern questions of culture that are transferred into questions of identity.

a. 180SearchAssistant
b. 6-3-5 Brainwriting
c. Power III
d. Cultural identity

7. _________ is the provision of service to customers before, during and after a purchase.

According to Turban et al., '_________ is a series of activities designed to enhance the level of customer satisfaction - that is, the feeling that a product or service has met the customer expectation.'

Its importance varies by product, industry and customer.

a. Customer experience
b. Facing
c. Customer service
d. COPC Inc.

8. _________ is an advertisement in which a particular product specifically mentions a competitor by name for the express purpose of showing why the competitor is inferior to the product naming it.

This should not be confused with parody advertisements, where a fictional product is being advertised for the purpose of poking fun at the particular advertisement, nor should it be confused with the use of a coined brand name for the purpose of comparing the product without actually naming an actual competitor. ('Wikipedia tastes better and is less filling than the Encyclopedia Galactica.')

In the 1980s, during what has been referred to as the cola wars, soft-drink manufacturer Pepsi ran a series of advertisements where people, caught on hidden camera, in a blind taste test, chose Pepsi over rival Coca-Cola.

a. Cost per conversion
b. GL-70
c. Heavy-up
d. Comparative advertising

1. The term _________ was first coined by New York Times best selling author, Linda Richardson. _________ emphasizes customer needs and meeting those needs with solutions combining products and/or services. A consultative salesperson typically provides detailed instruction or advice on which solution best meets these needs.

a. Sales management
b. Request for proposal
c. Lead generation
d. Consultative selling

2. _________ is the physical search for minerals, fossils, precious metals or mineral specimens, and is also known as fossicking.

_________ is synonymous in some ways with mineral exploration which is an organised, large scale and at least semi-scientific effort undertaken by mineral resource companies to find commercially viable ore deposits. To actually be considered a prospector you must become registered as a professional prospector.

a. Power III
b. 180SearchAssistant
c. Prospecting
d. 6-3-5 Brainwriting

3. In economics, business, retail, and accounting, a _________ is the value of money that has been used up to produce something, and hence is not available for use anymore. In economics, a _________ is an alternative that is given up as a result of a decision. In business, the _________ may be one of acquisition, in which case the amount of money expended to acquire it is counted as _________.

a. Transaction cost
b. Variable cost
c. Fixed costs
d. Cost

4. In the mathematical discipline of graph theory a _________ or edge-independent set in a graph is a set of edges without common vertices. It may also be an entire graph consisting of edges without common vertices.

Given a graph G = (V,E), a _________ M in G is a set of pairwise non-adjacent edges; that is, no two edges share a common vertex.

a. 6-3-5 Brainwriting
b. Matching
c. Power III
d. 180SearchAssistant

5. _________ is a form of social influence. It is the process of guiding people toward the adoption of an idea, attitude, or action by rational and symbolic (though not always logical) means. It is strategy of problem-solving relying on 'appeals' rather than coercion.

a. Power III
b. 180SearchAssistant
c. 6-3-5 Brainwriting
d. Persuasion

6. In operant conditioning, _________ occurs when an event following a response causes an increase in the probability of that response occurring in the future. Response strength can be assessed by measures such as the frequency with which the response is made (for example, a pigeon may peck a key more times in the session), or the speed with which it is made (for example, a rat may run a maze faster.) The environment change contingent upon the response is called a reinforcer.

a. Relationship Management Application
b. Generic brands
c. Completely randomized designs
d. Reinforcement

7. _________ is the identity of a group or culture, or of an individual as far as one is influenced by one's belonging to a group or culture. _________ is similar to and has overlaps with, but is not synonymous with, identity politics.

There are modern questions of culture that are transferred into questions of identity.

a. 180SearchAssistant
b. 6-3-5 Brainwriting
c. Cultural identity
d. Power III

8. _________ refers to the additional value of a commodity over the cost of commodities used to produce it from the previous stage of production. An example is the price of gasoline at the pump over the price of the oil in it. In national accounts used in macroeconomics, it refers to the contribution of the factors of production, i.e., land, labor, and capital goods, to raising the value of a product and corresponds to the incomes received by the owners of these factors. The factors of production provide 'services' which raise the unit price of a product (X) relative to the cost per unit of intermediate goods used up in the production of X. _________ is shared between the factors of production (capital, labor, also human capital), giving rise to issues of distribution.

a. Power III
b. Value added
c. Deregulation
d. Consumer spending

1. _________ is a term that refers both to:

- a formal discipline used to help appraise, or assess, the case for a project or proposal, which itself is a process known as project appraisal; and
- an informal approach to making decisions of any kind.

Under both definitions the process involves, whether explicitly or implicitly, weighing the total expected costs against the total expected benefits of one or more actions in order to choose the best or most profitable option. The formal process is often referred to as either CBA (_________) or BCost-benefit analysis

A hallmark of CBA is that all benefits and all costs are expressed in money terms, and are adjusted for the time value of money, so that all flows of benefits and flows of project costs over time (which tend to occur at different points in time) are expressed on a common basis in terms of their 'present value.' Closely related, but slightly different, formal techniques include Cost-effectiveness analysis, Economic impact analysis, Fiscal impact analysis and Social Return on Investment(SROI) analysis. The latter builds upon the logic of _________, but differs in that it is explicitly designed to inform the practical decision-making of enterprise managers and investors focused on optimising their social and environmental impacts.

a. Power III
b. 180SearchAssistant
c. 6-3-5 Brainwriting
d. Cost-benefit analysis

2. A personal and cultural _________ is a relative ethic _________, an assumption upon which implementation can be extrapolated. A _________ system is a set of consistent _________s and measures that is soo not true. A principle _________ is a foundation upon which other _________s and measures of integrity are based.

a. Perceptual maps
b. Value
c. Package-on-Package
d. Supreme Court of the United States

3. _________ is a branch of philosophy which seeks to address questions about morality, such as how a moral outcome can be achieved in a specific situation (applied _________), how moral values should be determined (normative _________), what moral values people actually abide by (descriptive _________), what the fundamental semantic, ontological, and epistemic nature of _________ or morality is (meta-_________), and how moral capacity or moral agency develops and what its nature is (moral psychology.)

Socrates was one of the first Greek philosophers to encourage both scholars and the common citizen to turn their attention from the outside world to the condition of man. In this view, Knowledge having a bearing on human life was placed highest, all other knowledge being secondary.

a. AMAX
b. ACNielsen
c. ADTECH
d. Ethics

4. _________ in organizations and public policy is both the organizational process of creating and maintaining a plan; and the psychological process of thinking about the activities required to create a desired goal on some scale. As such, it is a fundamental property of intelligent behavior. This thought process is essential to the creation and refinement of a plan, or integration of it with other plans, that is, it combines forecasting of developments with the preparation of scenarios of how to react to them.
a. 180SearchAssistant
b. Power III
c. 6-3-5 Brainwriting
d. Planning

5. A _________ is a plan of action designed to achieve a particular goal.

_________ is different from tactics. In military terms, tactics is concerned with the conduct of an engagement while _________ is concerned with how different engagements are linked.

a. 180SearchAssistant
b. 6-3-5 Brainwriting
c. Power III
d. Strategy

6. A _________ or pamphlet is a leaflet advertisement. _________s may advertise locations, events, hotels, products, services, etc. They are usually succinct in language and eye-catching in design.
a. Sweepstakes
b. Brochure
c. Customer relationship management
d. Marketspace

7. _________ is the identity of a group or culture, or of an individual as far as one is influenced by one's belonging to a group or culture. _________ is similar to and has overlaps with, but is not synonymous with, identity politics.

There are modern questions of culture that are transferred into questions of identity.

a. Cultural identity
b. 180SearchAssistant
c. 6-3-5 Brainwriting
d. Power III

8. _________ is a form of communication that typically attempts to persuade potential customers to purchase or to consume more of a particular brand of product or service. 'While now central to the contemporary global economy and the reproduction of global production networks, it is only quite recently that _________ has been more than a marginal influence on patterns of sales and production. The formation of modern _________ was intimately bound up with the emergence of new forms of monopoly capitalism around the end of the 19th and beginning of the 20th century as one element in corporate strategies to create, organize and where possible control markets, especially for mass produced consumer goods.
a. Advertising
b. ADTECH
c. ACNielsen
d. AMAX

1. _________ in economics and business is the result of an exchange and from that trade we assign a numerical monetary value to a good, service or asset. If I trade 4 apples for an orange, the _________ of an orange is 4 - apples. Inversely, the _________ of an apple is 1/4 oranges.

a. Contribution margin-based pricing
b. Pricing
c. Price
d. Discounts and allowances

2. A _________ is a collection of symbols, experiences and associations connected with a product, a service, a person or any other artifact or entity.

_________s have become increasingly important components of culture and the economy, now being described as 'cultural accessories and personal philosophies'.

Some people distinguish the psychological aspect of a _________ from the experiential aspect.

a. Brandable software
b. Brand equity
c. Store brand
d. Brand

3. _________ generally refers to a list of all planned expenses and revenues. It is a plan for saving and spending. A _________ is an important concept in microeconomics, which uses a _________ line to illustrate the trade-offs between two or more goods.

a. 180SearchAssistant
b. Power III
c. 6-3-5 Brainwriting
d. Budget

4. In economics, business, retail, and accounting, a _________ is the value of money that has been used up to produce something, and hence is not available for use anymore. In economics, a _________ is an alternative that is given up as a result of a decision. In business, the _________ may be one of acquisition, in which case the amount of money expended to acquire it is counted as _________.

a. Fixed costs
b. Variable cost
c. Transaction cost
d. Cost

5. _________ is the identity of a group or culture, or of an individual as far as one is influenced by one's belonging to a group or culture. _________ is similar to and has overlaps with, but is not synonymous with, identity politics.

There are modern questions of culture that are transferred into questions of identity.

a. 180SearchAssistant
b. 6-3-5 Brainwriting
c. Cultural identity
d. Power III

6. In promotion and of advertising, a _________ or endorsement consists of a written or spoken statement, sometimes from a person figure, sometimes from a private citizen, extolling the virtue of some product. The term '_________' most commonly applies to the sales-pitches attributed to ordinary citizens, whereas 'endorsement' usually applies to pitches by celebrities. See also Testify, Testimony, for historical context and etymology.

a. Testimonial
b. Transpromotional
c. Promotional products
d. Roll-in

7. The most important feature of a contract is that one party makes an _________ for an arrangement that another accepts. This can be called a 'concurrence of wills' or 'ad idem' (meeting of the minds) of two or more parties. The concept is somewhat contested.

a. ADTECH
b. ACNielsen
c. AMAX
d. Offer

8. _________ refer to a collection of facts usually collected as the result of experience, observation or experiment or a set of premises. This may consist of numbers, words particularly as measurements or observations of a set of variables. _________ are often viewed as a lowest level of abstraction from which information and knowledge are derived.

a. Sample size
b. Mean
c. Pearson product-moment correlation coefficient
d. Data

1. A personal and cultural _________ is a relative ethic _________, an assumption upon which implementation can be extrapolated. A _________ system is a set of consistent _________s and measures that is soo not true. A principle _________ is a foundation upon which other _________s and measures of integrity are based.

a. Package-on-Package
b. Perceptual maps
c. Supreme Court of the United States
d. Value

2. _________ is a branch of philosophy which seeks to address questions about morality, such as how a moral outcome can be achieved in a specific situation (applied _________), how moral values should be determined (normative _________), what moral values people actually abide by (descriptive _________), what the fundamental semantic, ontological, and epistemic nature of _________ or morality is (meta-_________), and how moral capacity or moral agency develops and what its nature is (moral psychology.)

Socrates was one of the first Greek philosophers to encourage both scholars and the common citizen to turn their attention from the outside world to the condition of man. In this view, Knowledge having a bearing on human life was placed highest, all other knowledge being secondary.

a. ADTECH
b. Ethics
c. ACNielsen
d. AMAX

3. A _________ is a collection of symbols, experiences and associations connected with a product, a service, a person or any other artifact or entity.

_________s have become increasingly important components of culture and the economy, now being described as 'cultural accessories and personal philosophies'.

Some people distinguish the psychological aspect of a _________ from the experiential aspect.

a. Brand equity
b. Store brand
c. Brand
d. Brandable software

4. A _________ is a business operated under a contract or license associated with a degree of exclusivity in business within a certain geographical area. For example, sports arenas or public parks may have _________ stands. Many department stores contain numerous _________s operated by other retailers.

a. Gross Margin Return on Inventory Investment
b. Concession
c. Strict liability
d. Promotion

5. In finance, an _________ is a contract between a buyer and a seller that gives the buyer the right--but not the obligation-- to buy or to sell a particular asset (the underlying asset) at a later day at an agreed price. In return for granting the _________, the seller collects a payment (the premium) from the buyer. A call _________ gives the buyer the right to buy the underlying asset; a put _________ gives the buyer of the _________ the right to sell the underlying asset.
a. Option
b. ACNielsen
c. AMAX
d. ADTECH

6. Importance of _________ is critical for any commercial organization. Expanding business is not possible without increasing sales volumes, and effective _________ goal is to organize sales team work in such a manner that ensures a growing flow of regular customers and increasing amount of sales.

The four phase-model of Management Process

1. Conception
2. Planning
3. Execution
4. Control

This model is cyclical, so it is a constant/continuous process.

===_________ is attainment of sales force goals in a effective ' efficient manner through planning, staffing, training, leading ' controlling organizational resources.

a. Hit rate
b. Sales process
c. Request for proposal
d. Sales management

7. _________ is a broad label that refers to any individuals or households that use goods and services generated within the economy. The concept of a _________ is used in different contexts, so that the usage and significance of the term may vary.

A _________ is a person who uses any product or service.

a. 180SearchAssistant
b. 6-3-5 Brainwriting
c. Consumer
d. Power III

8. _________ is the identity of a group or culture, or of an individual as far as one is influenced by one's belonging to a group or culture. _________ is similar to and has overlaps with, but is not synonymous with, identity politics.

There are modern questions of culture that are transferred into questions of identity.

a. 6-3-5 Brainwriting
b. Power III
c. 180SearchAssistant
d. Cultural identity

9. In operant conditioning, _________ occurs when an event following a response causes an increase in the probability of that response occurring in the future. Response strength can be assessed by measures such as the frequency with which the response is made (for example, a pigeon may peck a key more times in the session), or the speed with which it is made (for example, a rat may run a maze faster.) The environment change contingent upon the response is called a reinforcer.

a. Completely randomized designs
b. Reinforcement
c. Relationship Management Application
d. Generic brands

1. _________ is a contract between two parties, one being the employer and the other being the employee. An employee may be defined as: 'A person in the service of another under any contract of hire, express or implied, oral or written, where the employer has the power or right to control and direct the employee in the material details of how the work is to be performed.' Black's Law Dictionary page 471 (5th ed. 1979.)

a. ACNielsen
b. ADTECH
c. AMAX
d. Employment

2. _________ is the physical search for minerals, fossils, precious metals or mineral specimens, and is also known as fossicking.

_________ is synonymous in some ways with mineral exploration which is an organised, large scale and at least semi-scientific effort undertaken by mineral resource companies to find commercially viable ore deposits. To actually be considered a prospector you must become registered as a professional prospector.

a. Power III
b. 6-3-5 Brainwriting
c. 180SearchAssistant
d. Prospecting

3. In economics, business, retail, and accounting, a _________ is the value of money that has been used up to produce something, and hence is not available for use anymore. In economics, a _________ is an alternative that is given up as a result of a decision. In business, the _________ may be one of acquisition, in which case the amount of money expended to acquire it is counted as _________.

a. Transaction cost
b. Variable cost
c. Fixed costs
d. Cost

4. _________ is the provision of service to customers before, during and after a purchase.

According to Turban et al., '_________ is a series of activities designed to enhance the level of customer satisfaction - that is, the feeling that a product or service has met the customer expectation.'

Its importance varies by product, industry and customer.

a. COPC Inc.
b. Customer experience
c. Facing
d. Customer service

5. _________ is an advertisement in which a particular product specifically mentions a competitor by name for the express purpose of showing why the competitor is inferior to the product naming it.

This should not be confused with parody advertisements, where a fictional product is being advertised for the purpose of poking fun at the particular advertisement, nor should it be confused with the use of a coined brand name for the purpose of comparing the product without actually naming an actual competitor. ('Wikipedia tastes better and is less filling than the Encyclopedia Galactica.')

In the 1980s, during what has been referred to as the cola wars, soft-drink manufacturer Pepsi ran a series of advertisements where people, caught on hidden camera, in a blind taste test, chose Pepsi over rival Coca-Cola.

a. Comparative advertising
b. Heavy-up
c. Cost per conversion
d. GL-70

6. _________ is the identity of a group or culture, or of an individual as far as one is influenced by one's belonging to a group or culture. _________ is similar to and has overlaps with, but is not synonymous with, identity politics.

There are modern questions of culture that are transferred into questions of identity.

a. 180SearchAssistant
b. 6-3-5 Brainwriting
c. Power III
d. Cultural identity

7. A personal and cultural _________ is a relative ethic _________, an assumption upon which implementation can be extrapolated. A _________ system is a set of consistent _________s and measures that is soo not true. A principle _________ is a foundation upon which other _________s and measures of integrity are based.
a. Supreme Court of the United States
b. Perceptual maps
c. Package-on-Package
d. Value

8. _________ is a branch of philosophy which seeks to address questions about morality, such as how a moral outcome can be achieved in a specific situation (applied _________), how moral values should be determined (normative _________), what moral values people actually abide by (descriptive _________), what the fundamental semantic, ontological, and epistemic nature of _________ or morality is (meta-_________), and how moral capacity or moral agency develops and what its nature is (moral psychology.)

Socrates was one of the first Greek philosophers to encourage both scholars and the common citizen to turn their attention from the outside world to the condition of man. In this view, Knowledge having a bearing on human life was placed highest, all other knowledge being secondary.

a. ADTECH
b. ACNielsen
c. AMAX
d. Ethics

9. In operant conditioning, _________ occurs when an event following a response causes an increase in the probability of that response occurring in the future. Response strength can be assessed by measures such as the frequency with which the response is made (for example, a pigeon may peck a key more times in the session), or the speed with which it is made (for example, a rat may run a maze faster.) The environment change contingent upon the response is called a reinforcer.

a. Relationship Management Application
b. Generic brands
c. Completely randomized designs
d. Reinforcement

10. _________ is defined by the Oxford English Dictionary as 'the action or practice of selling among or between established clients, markets, traders, etc.' or 'that of selling an additional product or service to an existing customer'. In practice businesses define _________ in many different ways. Elements that might influence the definition might include: the size of the business, the industry sector it operates within and the financial motivations of those required to define the term.

a. Cross-selling
b. Yield management
c. Service provider
d. Freebie marketing

1. _________ refers to a range of skills, tools, and techniques utilized to accomplish specific tasks, projects and goals. This set encompass a wide scope of activities, and these include planning, setting goals, delegation, analysis of time spent, monitoring, organizing, scheduling, and prioritizing. Initially _________ referred to just business or work activities, but eventually the term broadened to include personal activities also.

a. Digital strategy
b. Goal setting
c. Business plan
d. Time Management

2. _________ in organizations and public policy is both the organizational process of creating and maintaining a plan; and the psychological process of thinking about the activities required to create a desired goal on some scale. As such, it is a fundamental property of intelligent behavior. This thought process is essential to the creation and refinement of a plan, or integration of it with other plans, that is, it combines forecasting of developments with the preparation of scenarios of how to react to them.

a. Power III
b. Planning
c. 180SearchAssistant
d. 6-3-5 Brainwriting

3. _________ is the identity of a group or culture, or of an individual as far as one is influenced by one's belonging to a group or culture. _________ is similar to and has overlaps with, but is not synonymous with, identity politics.

There are modern questions of culture that are transferred into questions of identity.

a. 6-3-5 Brainwriting
b. 180SearchAssistant
c. Power III
d. Cultural identity

4. _________ is the physical search for minerals, fossils, precious metals or mineral specimens, and is also known as fossicking.

_________ is synonymous in some ways with mineral exploration which is an organised, large scale and at least semi-scientific effort undertaken by mineral resource companies to find commercially viable ore deposits. To actually be considered a prospector you must become registered as a professional prospector.

a. 6-3-5 Brainwriting
b. Prospecting
c. Power III
d. 180SearchAssistant

5. In economics, business, retail, and accounting, a _________ is the value of money that has been used up to produce something, and hence is not available for use anymore. In economics, a _________ is an alternative that is given up as a result of a decision. In business, the _________ may be one of acquisition, in which case the amount of money expended to acquire it is counted as _________.
a. Cost
b. Variable cost
c. Fixed costs
d. Transaction cost

6. In accounting, _________ has a very specific meaning. It is an outflow of cash or other valuable assets from a person or company to another person or company. This outflow of cash is generally one side of a trade for products or services that have equal or better current or future value to the buyer than to the seller.
a. Expense
b. ACNielsen
c. AMAX
d. ADTECH

1. _________ is a contract between two parties, one being the employer and the other being the employee. An employee may be defined as: 'A person in the service of another under any contract of hire, express or implied, oral or written, where the employer has the power or right to control and direct the employee in the material details of how the work is to be performed.' Black's Law Dictionary page 471 (5th ed. 1979.)

a. ADTECH
b. AMAX
c. ACNielsen
d. Employment

2. _________ is a form of communication that typically attempts to persuade potential customers to purchase or to consume more of a particular brand of product or service. 'While now central to the contemporary global economy and the reproduction of global production networks, it is only quite recently that _________ has been more than a marginal influence on patterns of sales and production. The formation of modern _________ was intimately bound up with the emergence of new forms of monopoly capitalism around the end of the 19th and beginning of the 20th century as one element in corporate strategies to create, organize and where possible control markets, especially for mass produced consumer goods.

a. Advertising
b. ADTECH
c. ACNielsen
d. AMAX

3. _________ is the identity of a group or culture, or of an individual as far as one is influenced by one's belonging to a group or culture. _________ is similar to and has overlaps with, but is not synonymous with, identity politics.

There are modern questions of culture that are transferred into questions of identity.

a. 180SearchAssistant
b. 6-3-5 Brainwriting
c. Cultural identity
d. Power III

4. In economics, an externality or spillover of an economic transaction is an impact on a party that is not directly involved in the transaction. In such a case, prices do not reflect the full costs or benefits in production or consumption of a product or service. A positive impact is called an _________ benefit, while a negative impact is called an _________ cost.

a. AMAX
b. External
c. ACNielsen
d. ADTECH

5. _________ is the set of reasons that determines one to engage in a particular behavior. The term is generally used for human _________ but, theoretically, it can be used to describe the causes for animal behavior as well

a. Power III

b. Role playing

c. 180SearchAssistant

d. Motivation

Chapter 1

1. d 2. d 3. b 4. a 5. b 6. a 7. d 8. d 9. c 10. d
11. c 12. d 13. c 14. c

Chapter 2

1. d 2. a 3. a 4. a 5. c 6. a 7. c 8. d 9. c 10. d
11. c

Chapter 3

1. b 2. c 3. b 4. b 5. d 6. b 7. d

Chapter 4

1. d 2. c 3. a

Chapter 5

1. c 2. d 3. d 4. a 5. d 6. b 7. d 8. d 9. d 10. b

Chapter 6

1. d 2. d 3. d 4. d 5. b 6. b 7. b 8. d 9. a 10. d
11. d 12. d 13. b 14. a

Chapter 7

1. d 2. c 3. d 4. a 5. d 6. d 7. b 8. c 9. d 10. d
11. d 12. a 13. a

Chapter 8

1. b 2. d 3. a 4. b 5. a 6. a 7. b 8. d

Chapter 9

1. d 2. d 3. d 4. b 5. d 6. c 7. d 8. d 9. d 10. d

Chapter 10

1. d 2. d 3. c 4. b 5. d 6. d 7. c 8. d

Chapter 11

1. d 2. c 3. d 4. b 5. d 6. d 7. c 8. b

Chapter 12

1. d 2. b 3. d 4. d 5. d 6. b 7. a 8. a

Chapter 13

1. c 2. d 3. d 4. d 5. c 6. a 7. d 8. d

Chapter 14

1. d 2. b 3. c 4. b 5. a 6. d 7. c 8. d 9. b

Chapter 15

1. d 2. d 3. d 4. d 5. a 6. d 7. d 8. d 9. d 10. a

Chapter 16

1. d 2. b 3. d 4. b 5. a 6. a

Chapter 17

1. d 2. a 3. c 4. b 5. d

www.ingramcontent.com/pod-product-compliance
Lightning Source LLC
Chambersburg PA
CBHW080744250426
43671CB00038B/2859
* 9 7 8 1 4 2 8 8 7 2 0 1 1 *